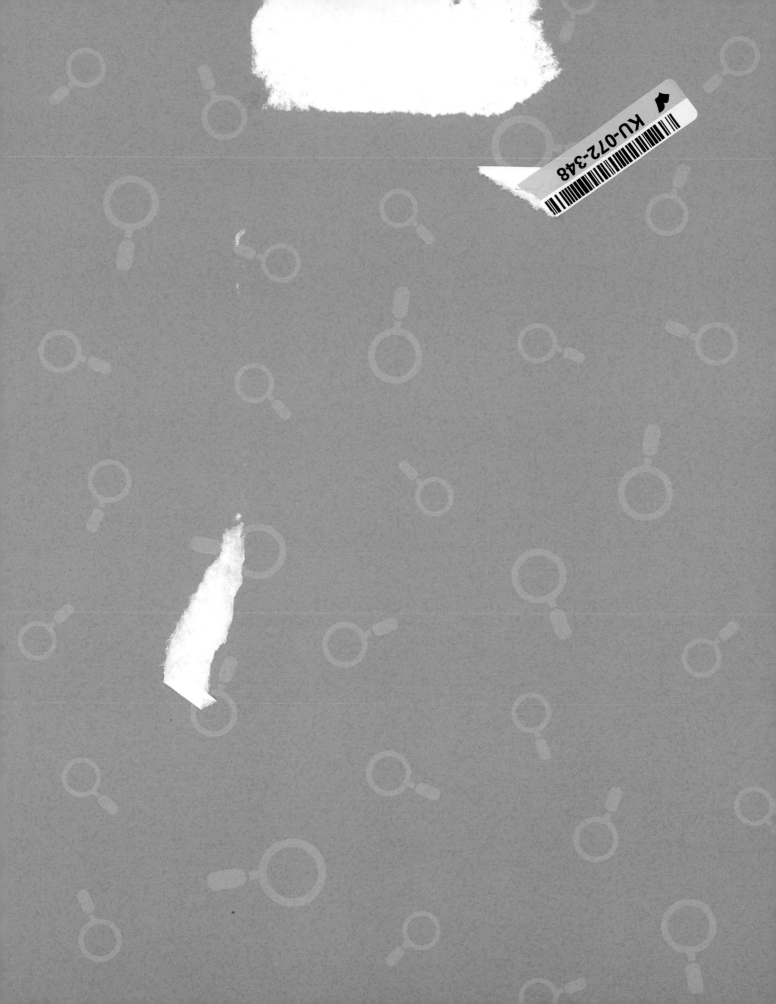

DISCOVER AND DO!

RIVERS

GET HANDS-ON WITH GEOGRAPHY

Written by Jane Lacey

W
FRANKLIN WATTS
LONDON • SYDNEY

Franklin Watts
First published in Great Britain in 2021
by The Watts Publishing Group
Copyright © The Watts Publishing Group, 2021

 Produced for Franklin Watts by
White-Thomson Publishing Ltd
www.wtpub.co.uk

Editor: Katie Dicker
Designer: Clare Nicholas
Series designer: Rocket Design (East Anglia) Ltd

Picture credits:
t=top b=bottom m=middle l=left r=right

Shutterstock: Robles Designery and GraphicsRF.com
cover/title page l, VitaminCo *cover/title page r*, Sky and
glass 4 and 10t, Maquiladora 5tl and 18b, aurielaki
5tr and 24t, KatyGr5 5br and 18tr, NEILRAS 6–7b,
StockBURIN 7t, ActiveLines 8t, 10b and 30t, stihii 9t,
humphery 12t, Catmando 12b, wickerwood 14m,
Oceloti 14b, maxstockphoto 15br, NotionPic 18tl,
A7880S 18m, Ronnie Howard 19t, MicroOne 20t,
Zentangle 20b and 31m, Leene 22t, Nikola Knezevic
22b, Parinya Panyana 24b and 31t, N.Savranska 26t
and 31b, intararit 26b, D L Kugler 27t, sutlafk 27b
and 32; Getty: hermandesign2015 5tl and 18b, ne2pi
6t, july7th 7m, corbac40 8b, Dorling Kindersley 14t,
erhui1979 16t and 30b, fona2 16b and 29t, Irina
Cheremisinova 18t and 28.

All design elements from Shutterstock.
Craft models from a previous series by Q2AMedia.

Every attempt has been made to clear copyright.
Should there be any inadvertent omission, please
apply to the publisher for rectification.

Printed in China

Franklin Watts
An imprint of
Hachette Children's Group
Part of The Watts Publishing Group
Carmelite House
50 Victoria Embankment
London EC4Y 0DZ

An Hachette UK Company
www.hachettechildrens.co.uk

DISCOVER AND DO!

RIVERS
GET HANDS-ON WITH GEOGRAPHY

W
FRANKLIN WATTS
LONDON • SYDNEY

CONTENTS

Words that appear in **bold** can be found in the glossary on pages 28–29.

WHAI IS A RIVER?

A river is a wide stream of water flowing downhill over land to the sea. Rivers flow along **channels** that can be straight or winding, wide or narrow, deep or shallow.

Rivers twist and turn as they make their way towards the sea.

Longest and biggest!

The world's longest river is the Nile River in Africa. It is 6,671 kilometres long. The Amazon River in South America is 6,440 kilometres long. Although it is the second longest river, the Amazon is the biggest because it holds the most water.

The Amazon River flows through thick rainforest to the sea. It pours 94 million litres of water into the Atlantic Ocean every second!

The water cycle

Rivers are part of the **water cycle**. When rain falls onto the land, some soaks into the ground or is taken in by plants. Rain water also collects in lakes and ponds, and flows from streams and rivers into the sea. When this water **evaporates**, it rises into the air where it forms clouds and falls back to the ground as rain, sleet or snow.

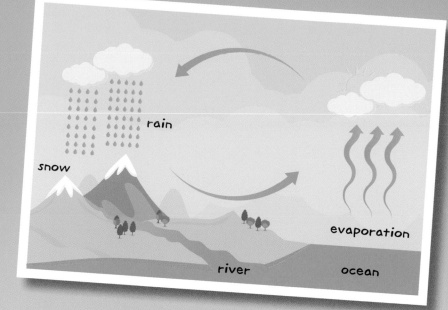

rain

snow

evaporation

river   ocean

Rivers play an important part in Earth's water cycle, returning rain water to the oceans.

Mountain streams run quickly over rocks down a mountain. They join together to form a river.

River water

The water that flows in rivers comes from rain water, melted snow and natural streams called **springs**. Small streams run downhill and join together to form rivers. Smaller rivers and streams that run into a bigger river are called **tributaries**.

ALL ALONG A RIVER

The force of **gravity** pulls things towards the centre of Earth. This makes river water flow downhill towards the sea. The flowing water is full of **energy** and constantly changes the shape and size of the river.

A river's course

The route of a river is called its course. It begins in high ground at the **source**. The highest part of a river, the upper course, is narrow and fast-flowing. In the middle course, the river becomes wider and deeper. In the lower course, the river flows more slowly, curving over flat ground.

The pull of gravity keeps water flowing downhill.

This diagram shows the three main stages of a river's course.

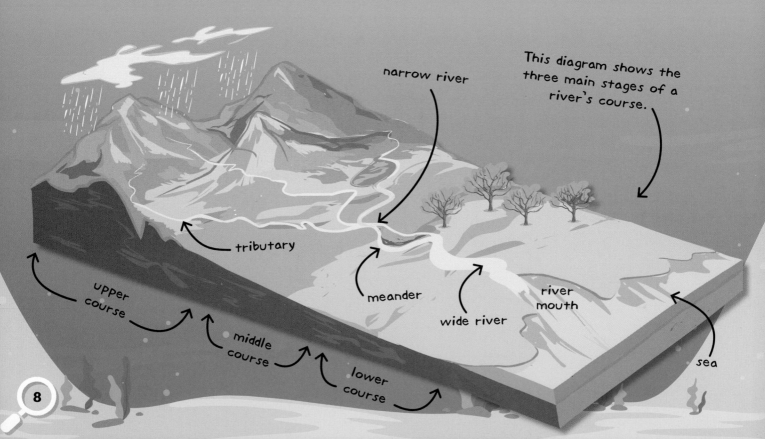

narrow river

tributary

meander

wide river

river mouth

upper course

middle course

lower course

sea

A river's mouth

The mouth of a river is where the water flows into the sea. This area is called an **estuary**. Some rivers drop **sediment** as they reach the sea. If the sediment splits the river into separate channels, a **delta** forms.

delta

This river has dropped sediment as it approaches the sea, creating a triangular-shaped delta.

ACTIVITY

MAKE A MODEL RIVER COURSE

You will need:
- **large rectangular tray**
- **self-hardening clay**
- **modelling tools to carve the clay**
- **waterproof paints**
- **jug of water**

1 At one end of the tray, build a clay mountain with steep slopes at the top, gentle slopes lower down and a flat base.

2 Carve a river course down your mountain. Make it narrow at the top and wider at the bottom. Add clay rocks for the river to flow over.

3 Paint your river course with blue and green paints, with some white or silver specks for foam and sunlight on the water. Leave to dry.

4 Pour water slowly into the top of your river course. Watch the water follow the course down the mountain.

WEARING AWAY THE LAND

Over many years, rivers **erode** the ground over which they flow. They can create deep channels called gorges or canyons, and dramatic waterfalls.

Gorges and canyons

Erosion takes place when river water carries along soil, sand and loose stones. These materials scrape and carve out the banks, or sides, of the river and the river bed, or bottom. Over many years, this makes the river deeper and wider.

The Colorado River helped to form the Grand Canyon in the USA over a period of 6 million years.

Waterfalls

Waterfalls usually form in the upper course of a river, where hard and soft rock meet. The fast-flowing water wears the soft rock away, leaving a ledge of hard rock. The river tumbles over the ledge to make a waterfall.

In a waterfall, the energy of the falling water may start to erode some of the hard rock too.

CREATE A COLLAGE WATERFALL

Ask an adult to help you with this activity

You will need:
- shoe box
- glue or sticky tape
- scissors
- waterproof paints
- green tissue paper
- plastic (from a large sandwich bag)
- bubble wrap

3 Cut the green tissue paper to make feathery ferns and water plants and glue them to the inside edges of the box.

1 Take the lid off the shoe box and put it over a narrow side of the box to make an L-shape. Glue or tape it in place. Ask an adult to cut the sides of the box to make it look like the edges of a river bank.

4 Cut the plastic into long ribbons and stick them to the top of the lid so they dangle down into the plunge pool and create a waterfall. You could add some bubble wrap to your pool to look like foam from the falling water.

2 Paint the box brown and green to look like rocks and plants around a waterfall. Paint the bottom (inside) green and blue for the plunge pool.

FLOOD PLAINS

Flood plains are found along the lower course of a river, where the water flows slowly and the land on either side is flat.

Rich farmland

When heavy rain falls, or water from melted snow flows down from the mountains, the river swells and overflows onto its flood plain. Sediment made up of sand, soil and bits of rock in the river water drops onto the ground, creating rich farmland.

The Yangtze River flood plain is good for growing rice.

Irrigation

The Nile River in Africa flows through areas of **desert**, where it hardly ever rains. Farmers store the river water in **irrigation** channels. They use it to water their crops throughout the year.

The Nile River is an important source of water for farmers in Egypt.

ACTIVITY

MAKE A SELF-WATERING SYSTEM

Ask an adult to help you with this activity

You will need:
- **small plastic water bottle**
- **duct tape**
- **felt-tip pen**
- **square of plastic about 10 cm x 10 cm (from a strong plastic bag)**
- **pin**
- **elastic band**
- **pot plant in soil**
- **water**

3 Put the plastic over the bottle spout and secure it in place with an elastic band.

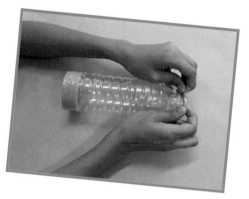

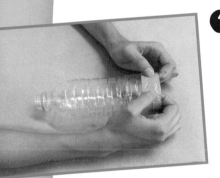

1 Remove the plastic lid from the bottle. Ask an adult to cut off the bottom of the bottle and to put duct tape over the sharp edge.

4 Turn the bottle upside down and push it into the soil next to the plant you need to water. Fill the bottle with water.

Your self-watering system stores water and helps to water your plant gradually. This is particularly useful if you have to go away for a few days. You could use larger bottles for outdoor plants.

2 Draw around the bottle spout onto the square of plastic with the felt-tip pen. Ask an adult to make four or five small holes in the plastic circle with the pin.

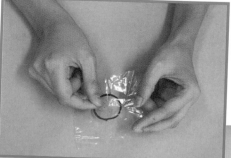

BENDS AND LOOPS

If you follow a river's course on a map, you will see that it does not travel in a straight line. As the river gets bigger, it bends and loops as the water weaves from side to side.

sediment

erosion

The speed at which a river flows around a bend causes erosion or sediment to form.

Meandering along

Meanders are bends in a river. The flow of water (the **current**) is faster around the outside of a bend and wears away the bank. On the inside of a bend, the slower current drops sediment and makes the bend bigger.

Oxbow lake

As the bends of a meander get bigger, they move towards each other. Sometimes the two bends meet and the river begins to flow between them. When this happens, the bend is cut off from the river and forms an oxbow lake.

The bends in a river can become so big that an oxbow lake forms.

PLAY 'POOH STICKS'

Use this activity to find out which parts of a river have the strongest current.

Two adults must be present during this activity at all times

You will need:
- **a friend**
- **two adults**
- **stopwatch**

1 Visit a small river or stream near to where you live, with a footbridge crossing over it.

2 Find two sticks. Push each stick through a large leaf to make them easy to recognise.

3 Mark a place about 20 metres downstream in the direction that the current is flowing. Make sure the bridge is still visible from this position. Ask your friend and an adult to stand by the mark with a stopwatch.

4 With an adult, take the sticks to the bridge. Shout 'Go!' as you drop one stick into the middle of the river and your friend starts the stopwatch.

5 How long does the stick take to reach the mark? Drop the other stick nearer the bank and do the same. Where is the current strongest? You could record your findings on a chart.

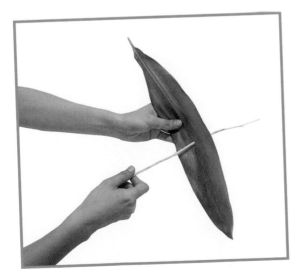

RIVER PLANTS

Many different kinds of plants grow in river beds, along river banks or in river water. Plants grow best in a slow-flowing river. A fast current may wash away soil and the plants that grow in it.

Some birds like to live and nest amongst the reeds by a river bank.

Along the banks

Willow trees often grow along river banks because they need to drink plenty of water. Their roots help to stop the banks eroding. When tall reeds grow close together by the river bank, they provide shelter for birds and river **mammals**.

Water lilies have long stems and flat leaves that float on the water to face the sunlight.

reeds

Plants in the water

Some water plants keep the river water healthy and full of **oxygen**. In fast-flowing water, plants growing up from the river bed have long, flexible stems. In slow-flowing water, some plants have flat leaves that float on the surface.

PAINT A RIVER PLANT PICTURE

Ask an adult to help you with this activity

You will need:
- **large sheet of paper**
- **several small sheets of paper**
- **pencil**
- **paints**

1 With an adult, visit a local river (or research a river on the Internet) to learn about the plants that grow there. If you arrange a visit, you can sketch your river and the plants you see (or you could take photographs).

2 Paint a stretch of the river and the river banks on a large sheet of paper.

3 Paint the river plants on the small pieces of paper (or print your photographs). Use books or the Internet to find out the names of the plants.

4 Stick the plant pictures around the edge of your river painting and label them clearly. Draw arrows to show where the plants are found.

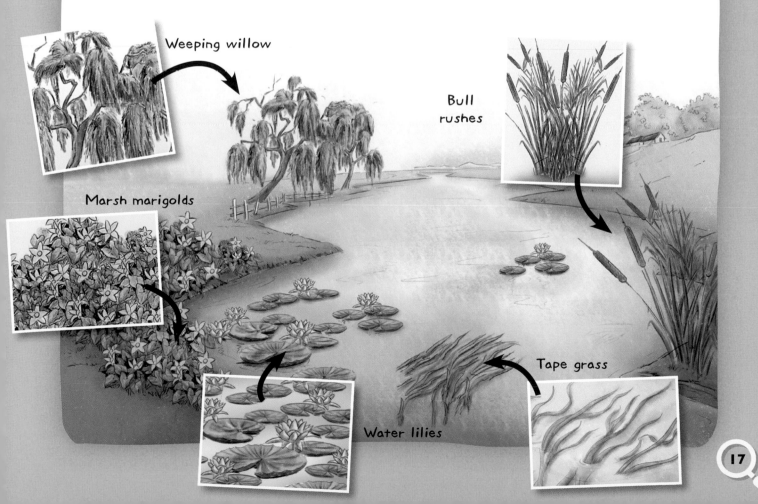

Weeping willow

Bull rushes

Marsh marigolds

Tape grass

Water lilies

RIVER WILDLIFE

Rivers provide food and shelter for all kinds of animals – fish, birds, **amphibians**, **reptiles**, mammals and insects. If there is a lot of wildlife using the river, it usually means that the water is clean and healthy.

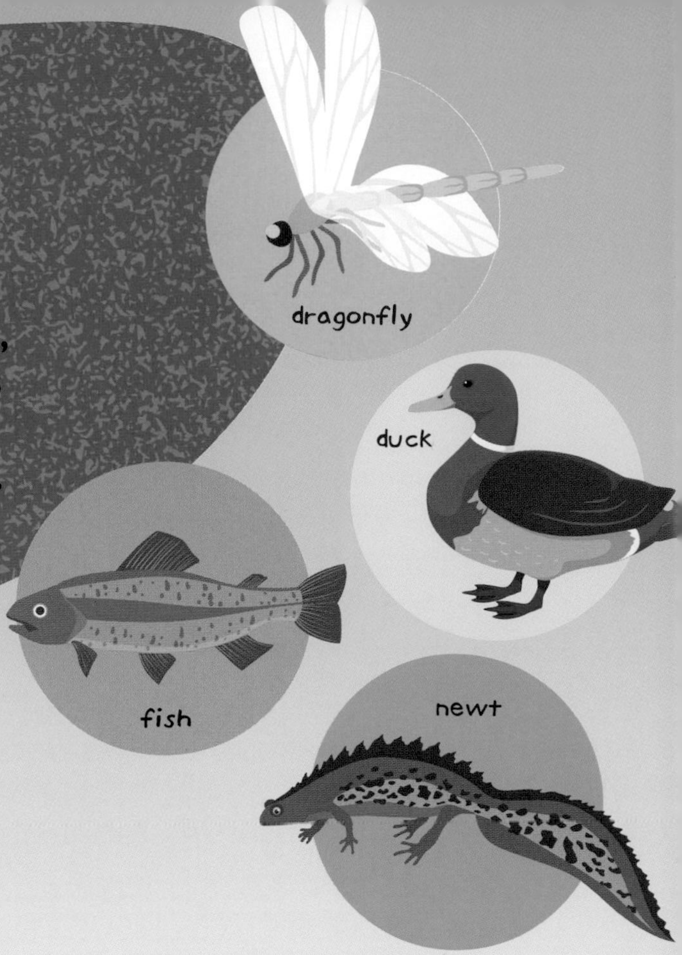

dragonfly

duck

fish

newt

On land and in the water

Frogs and toads are amphibians that live in the water and on land. You might see them swimming in the water, hopping on the bank or sitting on a water lily leaf. They lay hundreds of eggs, called spawn, in the water that hatch into new frogs. Some spawn are eaten by fish and birds.

Frogs make their home in a river or a pond. Their eggs hatch in the spring.

Mammals

Otters and beavers are river mammals. They dig their burrows in the banks of a river. Otters catch fish, frogs and birds to eat. Beavers eat the bark from trees. They use their sharp, strong teeth to drag branches into the water to build a dam.

Beavers build dams to block flowing river water. The dams make large, safe pools for them to swim in.

MAKE A BEAVER'S DAM

You will need:
- **deep rectangular tray**
- **stones and sticks**
- **self-hardening clay**
- **jug of water**
- **sheet of A3 paper**
- **paints or coloured pencils**

1 Build a wall with stones and sticks, about a third of the way along the tray.

2 Use the clay to fill any gaps. Leave a small hole in the middle of the dam for the water to trickle through.

3 Pour water slowly into the smaller space behind the dam and watch it collect to form a pool.

4 Paint or draw a backdrop for your dam on the paper, showing a forest with a family of beavers living there. Place it behind the dam.

USING RIVERS

People have always lived by rivers. River water can be used for drinking and for washing. Farmers use it to water their crops. A healthy river is also full of fish to eat.

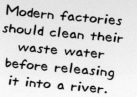

Factories

Many factories are built on the banks of rivers. The river water is used to help make **goods**. But the waste water these factories produce can be full of chemicals. If it is poured back into the river, it will cause harm.

Modern factories should clean their waste water before releasing it into a river.

Water power

Flowing river water is full of energy that can be captured and used to make **electricity**. A concrete dam is built to store river water. Jets of water flow through spaces in the dam and turn **turbines** that help to make electricity.

Water is stored by a dam at this power station to help make electricity.

MAKE A WATER FILTER

Ask an adult to help you with this activity

You will need:
- **large plastic bottle**
- **scissors**
- **duct tape**
- **paper kitchen towel**
- **sand**
- **gravel**
- **cotton-wool balls**
- **cooking oil**
- **selection of foodstuffs (such as rice, oatmeal and tea leaves)**
- **jug of water**
- **spoon**

1 Ask an adult to help you cut the plastic bottle in half and put duct tape over the sharp edges. Take off the cap.

2 Put the top half of the bottle upside down into the bottom half to make a funnel. Add layers of filter materials to your funnel in the following order – a paper kitchen towel, a layer of sand, a layer of gravel, some cotton-wool balls.

3 Add a tablespoon of cooking oil and the foodstuffs to a jug of water and stir. Pour the mixture slowly through the filter.

The filter helps to separate out some of the foodstuffs. How clean is the water that comes through the filter?

21

RIVER TRANSPORT

Rivers are natural routes that can be used to transport people and goods. Wide, deep and very long rivers help ships and boats to travel inland. They load and unload at **ports** along the banks of the river.

Light birch bark canoes can be easily transported.

River boats

Rivers have always been a popular place for people to settle, with transport so close to home. Many years ago, rafts, boats and canoes were only made from local materials. In Canada, for example, strong, light canoes were built from the soft bark of birch trees.

Canals

Canals are man-made rivers. They were dug between towns and used to join-up rivers before railways became a popular form of transport. Horses walked along **towpaths** to pull barges loaded with coal or other goods.

In Amsterdam, boats transport people and goods along the city's 165 canals.

MAKE A BIRCH BARK CANOE

You will need:
- **A4 thin brown card or strong paper**
- **pencil**
- **scissors**
- **hole punch**
- **string**
- **thick card**
- **glue or sticky tape**
- **felt-tip pens**

1 Fold the thin brown card in half lengthways. Draw a line 2 cm above the centre fold. Fold back one side of the card along this line. Turn the card over and repeat.

2 Turn the card so the folds are along the bottom (in a kind of W-shape but with the middle fold much shorter). Flatten and draw a canoe shape on the side. Make sure the bottom edge of the card is the bottom of your canoe. Cut it out.

3 Punch four holes along each end. Thread the string through the holes and secure tightly.

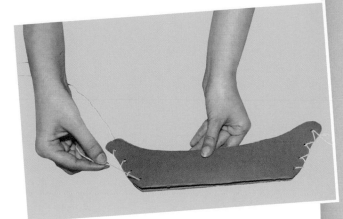

4 Push down the centre fold to give your canoe a flat bottom. Cut two small strips of card and tape or glue them across the top of your canoe to make two seals.

5 Decorate your canoe with felt-tip pens. Cut out a paddle from the thick card, to match your canoe. Pretend to float your canoe and carry it over different obstacles.

ENJOYING RIVERS

There are lots of things to enjoy by a river, from rowing in a boat to walking along the bank. There are fish to catch in the water and water birds to spot in the plants and trees.

In rowing competitions, strong rowers race along a river.

River sports

Many people enjoy river sports to get fit and to have fun. Skilled sports include paddling canoes or rowing boats (with up to eight rowers) along straight, flat stretches of river.

White water

Rivers tumble downhill over ridges and boulders, sending up spray and foam and creating 'white water'. People put on life jackets and go down the white water in rafts or canoes for a thrilling ride.

An inflatable white-water raft twists and turns along a raging river.

ACTIVITY

PLAY THE RIVER RACE BOARD GAME

You will need:
- 1 die
- small counters
- 2 or more players!

Take it in turns to roll the die and move your counters across the squares on this page. Follow the instructions on the squares you land on. The first to get to the sea is the winner!

Can you make a river race board game of your own?

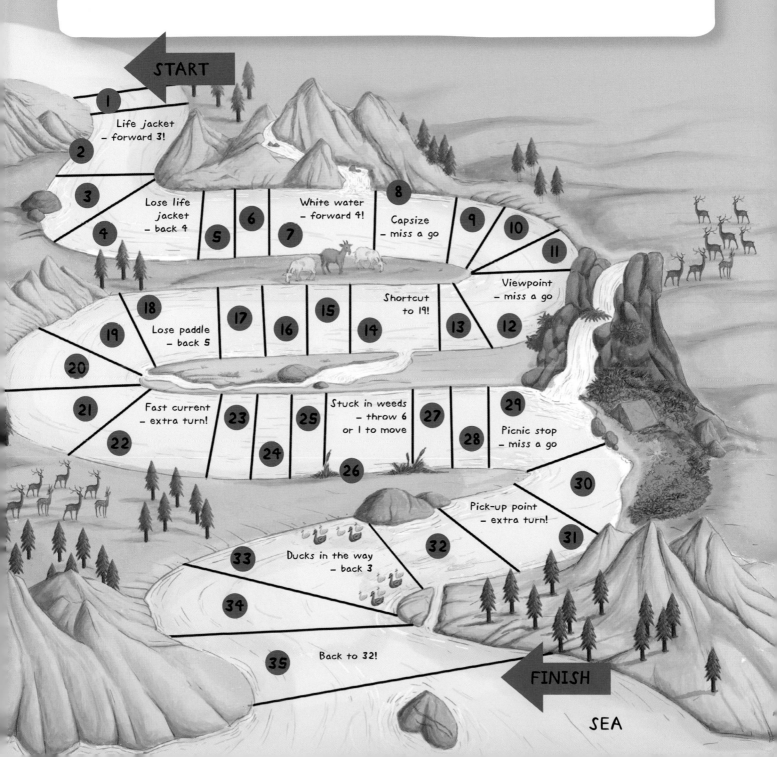

START

1

Life jacket – forward 3!

2

3

4

Lose life jacket – back 4

5

6

7

White water – forward 4!

8

Capsize – miss a go

9

10

11

Viewpoint – miss a go

12

13

Shortcut to 19!

14

15

16

17

18

Lose paddle – back 5

19

20

21

22

Fast current – extra turn!

23

24

25

Stuck in weeds – throw 6 or 1 to move

26

27

28

29

Picnic stop – miss a go

30

31

Pick-up point – extra turn!

32

33

Ducks in the way – back 3

34

35

Back to 32!

FINISH

SEA

CARING FOR RIVERS

Pollution and litter can harm rivers and the wildlife that depend on them. If some river plants grow too thick, they stop other wildlife growing. Everyone can get involved in keeping their local river clean and healthy.

Litter

Rivers and their banks are often used as dumping grounds for car tyres, shopping trolleys, traffic cones and other rubbish. Crisp packets and plastic bottles thrown away carelessly can clog up the water flow and harm river wildlife.

We can all do our bit to keep local rivers clean.

Waste and debris can pollute rivers in urban areas.

Harmful plants

Some river plants have been introduced from other countries. They can grow thick and tall, killing **native** plants and harming wildlife. Getting to know harmful plants and reporting them helps to control their growth.

Japanese knotweed grows on European river banks. It prevents the growth of native plants, erodes the banks and can cause flooding.

ACTIVITY

ADOPT A LOCAL RIVER

Ask an adult to help you with this activity

1 With the help of an adult, get to know your nearest river and the plants and animals that live there.

2 Draw sketches or take photographs of the plants and animals that you see.

3 Find out about an organisation that cares for the river (such as www.rivercare.org.uk). Join-up yourself, or find out if your school can get involved. Help out with one of their projects to look after the river, or another river nearby.

Glossary

amphibian

An amphibian is an animal that lives in water and on land.

channel

A channel is a trench or groove cut into the land. River water flows along channels.

current

A current is the continuous movement of water in a particular direction.

delta

A delta is a flat, swampy area of land at a river's mouth. It is made when a river drops sediment as it approaches the sea.

desert

A desert is a rocky or sandy area of land with little rainfall.

electricity

Electricity is a kind of energy made in power stations. We use electricity in our homes to turn on lights and to work machines.

energy

Energy is the power to work. River water has lots of energy.

erode

Erode means to wear away.

estuary

An estuary is the mouth of a river, where river water mixes with sea water.

evaporates

Water evaporates when it turns into a gas called water vapour.

flood plain

A flood plain is an area of low-lying ground next to a river, mainly formed from river sediment.

goods

Goods are items such as food or building materials that we transport from place to place.

gravity

Gravity is a force that pulls objects towards Earth's centre.

irrigation

Irrigation is the supplying of water to crops growing in dry fields.

mammal

Mammals are animals with fur or hair. Mammal mothers feed their babies with their own milk.

native

Native plants or animals come from a particular place and have not come from elsewhere.

oxygen

Oxygen is a gas that almost all living things need to survive.

pollution

Pollution is when something is made dirty. River water can become polluted with litter or harmful chemicals.

port

A port is a place by the coast or a river bank where boats can load and unload people and goods.

reptile

A reptile has scaly skin and cold blood. Reptiles, such as snakes and crocodiles, need heat from the Sun to warm them up.

sediment

Sediment is the bits of earth and rock carried by river water.

source

The source of a river is the point where it begins.

spring

A spring is where water bubbles up from underground.

towpath

A towpath is a path beside the bank of a river or canal.

tributaries

Tributaries are rivers or streams that join a bigger river.

turbines

Turbines are wheels turned by flowing water or air to make energy.

water cycle

The water on Earth goes round and round in a water cycle. Water falls as rain and runs into rivers and the sea. The water evaporates to make clouds and falls again as rain.

Quiz

1 The world's longest river is:

a) The Amazon
b) The Nile
c) The Yangtze
d) The Congo

2 Smaller rivers that run into a bigger river are called:

a) tributes
b) tribunes
c) tributaries
d) tripartites

3 In the upper course, a river:

a) is curved and moves slowly
b) is curved and moves fast
c) is narrow and moves slowly
d) is narrow and moves fast

4 A delta is shaped like a:

a) circle
b) square
c) rectangle
d) triangle

5 Waterfalls usually form in the:

a) upper course of a river
b) middle course of a river
c) lower course of a river
d) all parts of a river

6 Flood plains form in the:

a) upper course of a river
b) middle course of a river
c) lower course of a river
d) all parts of a river

7 River water flows faster around:

a) the outside of a bend
b) the inside of a bend
c) both sides of a bend
d) only in the middle

8 Plants grow best in:

a) a fast-flowing river
b) a slow-flowing river
c) a deep river
d) any type of river

9 Electricity generated by flowing water is called:

a) hydropower
b) superpower
c) power flow
d) energy flow

10 Which of the following are a type of river boat?

a) raft
b) canoe
c) barge
d) kayak

FURTHER INFORMATION

BOOKS

Geographics: Rivers and Coasts by Izzi Howell, Franklin Watts

Geographics: The Water Cycle by Georgia Amson-Bradshaw, Franklin Watts

The Where on Earth? Book of Rivers by Susie Brooks, Wayland

World Feature Focus: Rivers by Rebecca Kahn, Franklin Watts

WEBSITES

All about rivers and how they form www.bbc.co.uk/bitesize/topics/z849q6f/articles/z7w8pg8

A scientist helps to explain the definition of a river www.youtube.com/watch?v=7kgQNRQjIUU

Fascinating facts about rivers www.natgeokids.com/uk/home-is-good/fascinating-facts-about-rivers

Find out more and test yourself www.dkfindout.com/uk/earth/rivers

Index

Titles in the DISCOVER AND DO! GEOGRAPHY series

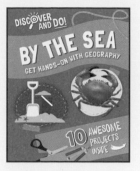

- The seashore
- Coasts
- Harbours
- Tides
- Wearing away
- Building beaches
- Human changes
- Enjoying the sea
- Fishing
- Seaside holidays
- Caring for the seaside

- Planet Earth
- Water
- Where I live
- Travelling around
- Litter
- Reduce, re-use!
- Recycle!
- Pollution
- Local wildlife
- Habitats
- Energy

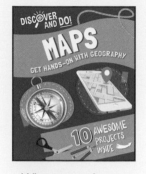

- What is a map?
- Bird's-eye view
- Symbols
- Making maps
- Compass points
- Map lines
- Scale
- Landscapes
- Plans
- Finding the way
- Planning a walk

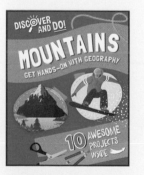

- What are mountains?
- Mountain types
- Erosion
- Volcanoes
- Mountain weather
- Mountain zones
- Mountain plants
- Mountain animals
- Living in the mountains
- Tourism
- Caring for mountains

- What is a river?
- All along a river
- Wearing away the land
- Flood plains
- Bends and loops
- River plants
- River wildlife
- Using rivers
- River transport
- Enjoying rivers
- Caring for rivers

- What is weather?
- Temperature
- Atmosphere
- Wind
- Water
- Storm!
- Extreme weather
- Weather forecasting
- Weather and lifestyles
- Adapting to weather
- Changing climates

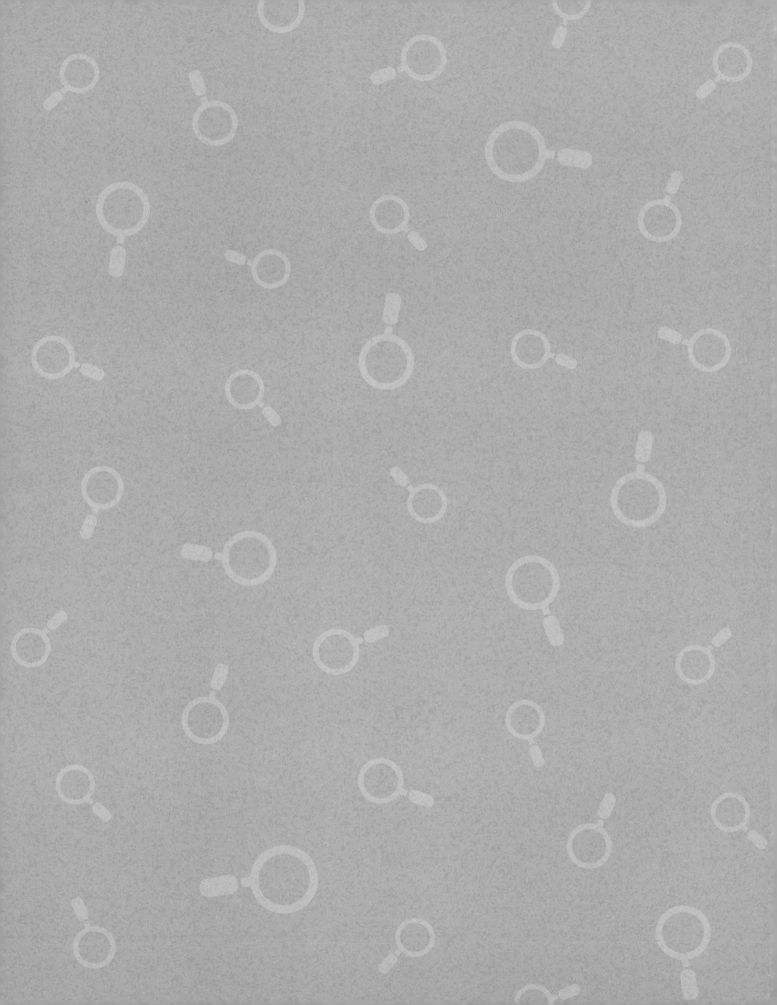

FIRST FESTIVALS

Christmas

Lois Rock

LION
Children's Books

This edition copyright © 1999 Lion Publishing
Illustrations copyright © 1999 Helen Cann
Music arrangements copyright © 1998 Philip Tebbs,
typeset by MSS Studios, Gwynedd
Photography by John Williams Studios, Thame
Text and artefacts by Lois Rock

The moral rights of the author and illustrator
have been asserted

Published by
Lion Publishing plc
Sandy Lane West, Oxford, England
www.lion-publishing.co.uk
ISBN 0 7459 3907 4

First edition 1999
10 9 8 7 6 5 4 3 2 1 0

A catalogue record for this book is available
from the British Library

Typeset in 18/21 Baskerville MT Schlbk
Printed and bound in Singapore

Acknowledgments
Bible passage on page 1 from Isaiah 9:2, 6–7. Scriptures
quoted from the Good News Bible published by The Bible
Societies/HarperCollins Publishers Ltd, UK © American Bible
Society 1966, 1971, 1976, 1992, used with permission.

Introduction

This book is one of a series dealing with the Christian festivals.

This one is about the best-loved of them all: the celebration of Christmas.

Here are traditional crafts to mark the season, from the looking-forward time of Advent to Christmas Day itself, with its gifts, greetings cards and decorations.

Here, too, is the story of the Nativity that lies at the heart of the festival, carols that sing out the story of Jesus' birth and tales from the Christian tradition that have shaped the customs of the season.

Contents

Advent

November nights are long and dark; in December, the nights are even longer.

As wintertime grows cold and bleak, those people who celebrate Christmas begin to look forward to a festive time at the end of the year: a celebration that is full of light and warmth and cheerfulness.

Christians call this season of waiting 'Advent'—a word which means 'coming'.

Advent begins four Sundays before Christmas.

As the weeks of Advent go by, Christians remember stories of long ago—stories of the Jewish people. Then, the Jews were a people who had been beaten in many wars. They were no longer free in the land they called their home. They believed that God had promised to send a special king who would lead them to freedom.

The coming of that king would be like a celebration after a long, dark winter.

A promise of a king

The people who walked in darkness have seen a great light.
They lived in a land of shadows, but now light is shining on them.
A child is born to us!
A son is given to us!
And he will be our ruler.
He will be called 'Wonderful Counsellor', 'Mighty God', 'Eternal Father',
    'Prince of Peace'.
His royal power will continue to grow; his kingdom will always be at peace.

From the book of the prophet Isaiah, in the Bible

2 Advent Ring

Here is a traditional Christian decoration for Advent. It helps count the four Sundays in Advent that lead up to Christmas.

On the first Sunday, people light one candle in the ring. As it burns, they may read or remember some of the words from the Bible in which God promises to send a king who will set people free.

On the second Sunday, they light two candles; on the third, they light three, and on the fourth they light four.

On Christmas Day, they light the centre candle as they remember the birth of the one they believe was God's king— the one they call 'Christ', the baby Jesus.

You will need

large garden saucer

damp soil or sand

5 small flowerpots

4 red candles

1 tall white candle

sprigs of evergreens such as fir, holly and ivy

1 Fill the garden saucer with soil or sand. Wedge four flowerpots in a circle around the edge, and another in the centre. Half fill these with soil or sand.

2 Put the red candles in the pots round the edge, and the white candle in the centre pot.

3 Push evergreen sprigs into the sand to cover it. Take care to keep the leaves below the rim of the pots, so they will not catch fire as the candles burn.

3 Advent Calendar

An Advent calendar helps count the days to Christmas. This one, like many, counts from 1 December to Christmas Day on 25 December.

There is a hidden surprise for every day in Advent.

1 Draw a simple Christmas tree shape. The one here was 70 cm tall including the pot. Ask a grown-up to help you cut it out, using a craft knife against a ruler on a cutting mat.

2 Mark equally spaced lines to show where the yarn will go. Cut notches where these lines meet the edge of the tree.

3 Paint the tree green and the pot red. Leave to dry.

4 Wind fuzzy yarn around the tree, using the notches as guides. Hold the beginning and end of the yarn in place with sticky tape on the wrong side of the card.

You will need

large sheet of thick card

pencil and ruler

cutting mat and craft knife

green and red acrylic paint

paintbrushes

fuzzy yarn

sticky tape

scissors

This Advent calendar is shaped like a Christmas tree. The plain envelopes each contain a paper decoration. Unwrap one decoration each day and hang it on the tree.

Make an extra special star to put on the top for Christmas Day. Use tape or sticky putty to hold it in place.

4 Decorations

Here's how to make bright decorations and envelopes for your Advent calendar tree.

Decorations

You will need

thin card

pencil

scissors

strong paper in lots of bright colours

coloured yarn

sticky tape

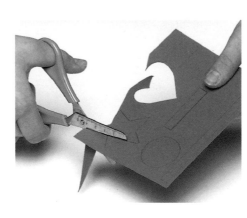

1 Draw shapes like the ones shown here onto thin card and cut them out. Use the templates at the back of this book as guides.

2 One at a time, hold a shape against a piece of strong paper and tear it little by little along the edges to get the same shape. Tear out all the shapes you need to make 25 decorations!

3 Glue the shapes together to make decorations.

4 Cut yarn in 15 cm lengths and fold each in half. Tape a piece to each decoration on the wrong side, with the cut ends free so you can tie the decoration onto your tree.

Envelopes

You will need

large sheets of red paper

gold coloured paper-clips

ruler and pencil

scissors

gold pen

gold stickers

1 Use a ruler and pencil to mark squares on the red paper. The squares for the envelopes shown here were 9 cm x 9 cm.

2 Place a ruler along each line and tear the paper firmly along it. Tear the marked paper first into strips, and then the strips into mini squares.

3 Fold each square in half and in half again. Hold the folded paper with the central point towards you, and snip a tiny piece off the two side corners but not the top one.

4 Unfold it. There will be a notch in the middle of each side. Lay your decoration in the centre of the square, then fold in each point over it, folding from notch to notch.

5 Sticker the envelope shut to hold the points together.

6 Number each envelope from 1 to 25. You are now ready to hang them on the tree in order, from the bottom of the tree to the top, using a paper-clip on the yarn (see the picture on page 3).

5 The Christmas Story

The story at the heart of Christmas is the story of the birth of Jesus. The people who believe he was God's special king—the Christ—call themselves Christians. Christmas ('Christ-mas') is the name of their festival.

Mary and the angel

Long ago, in the town of Nazareth in Palestine, lived a young woman named Mary. Like all the girls her age, she was planning to get married. The man who was going to be her husband was called Joseph.

One day, an angel appeared to Mary. 'Greetings,' said the angel. 'I bring special news. God has chosen you to bear a child—the king for

whom your people are waiting. You are to call him Jesus.'

Mary was puzzled and dismayed. 'How can I be a mother?' she asked. 'I'm not yet a wife!'

'God can make this come true,' said the angel; and Mary agreed to do as God wanted.

The birth of Jesus

Months went by. The time was coming when Mary's baby would be born. Then came an announcement from the emperor who ruled the land. He wanted to know exactly how many people lived in his empire, so he could ask them to pay taxes. Everyone was ordered to go to their home town to put their names on a list.

So Joseph took Mary from Nazareth to Bethlehem. Many people were travelling for the same reason. In crowded Bethlehem, the only place where Mary and Joseph could find shelter was a stable.

There, Mary's baby was born. Mary wrapped the child in swaddling bands and laid him to sleep in a manger.

Away in a Manger

A-way in a — man-ger, no — crib for a bed, The — lit-tle Lord Je-sus laid — down his sweet head. The — stars in the — bright sky looked — down where he lay, The — lit-tle Lord Je-sus a-sleep on the hay.

The cattle are lowing, the baby awakes,
But little Lord Jesus, no crying he makes.
I love thee, Lord Jesus! Look down from the sky,
And stay by my side until morning is nigh.

Be near me, Lord Jesus, I ask thee to stay
Close by me for ever, and love me, I pray.
Bless all the dear children in thy tender care,
And fit us for heaven to live with thee there.

6 The Christmas Story

The shepherds on the hillside

On the same night that Mary's baby was born, there were some shepherds out on the hillside near Bethlehem. They were watching over their sheep.

Suddenly, an angel appeared. The shepherds were terrified.

'Do not be afraid,' said the angel. 'I bring you good news, and the good news is for everyone. You know that Bethlehem is the town where your great King David was born, long ago. Tonight, God's special king has been born there: the Christ has come.

'Go and find out for yourselves that what I am saying is true. You will find the baby wrapped in swaddling bands and lying in a manger.'

Then a great crowd of angels appeared. They sang songs of praise:

'Glory to God in the highest, and peace on earth.'

When the angels had gone, the shepherds looked at one another in amazement. 'Let us go to Bethlehem, and see what has happened,' they said.

So they went, and they found Mary and the baby, just as the angel had said.

While Shepherds Watched Their Flocks

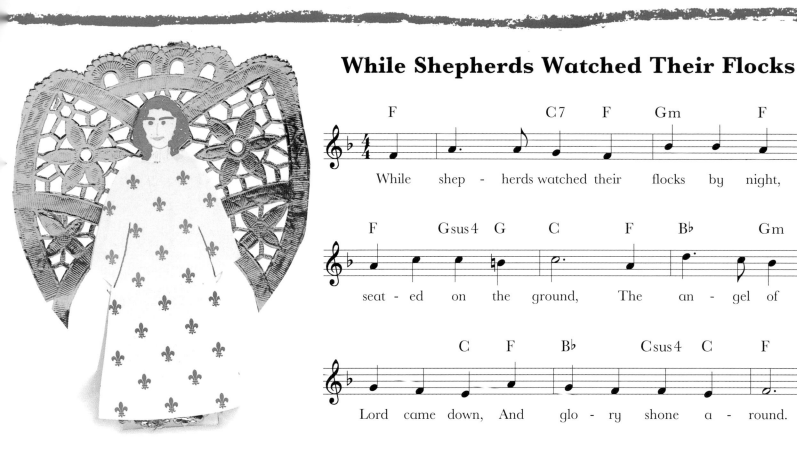

While shep-herds watched their flocks by night, All
seat-ed on the ground, The an-gel of the
Lord came down, And glo-ry shone a-round.

'Fear not,' said he, for mighty dread
Had seized their troubled mind;
'Glad tidings of great joy I bring
To you and all mankind.

'To you in David's town this day
Is born of David's line
A saviour who is Christ the Lord;
And this shall be the sign:

'The heavenly babe you there shall find
To human view displayed,
All meanly wrapped in swathing bands,
And in a manger laid.'

Thus spake the seraph and forthwith
Appeared a shining throng
Of angels praising God, who thus
Addressed their joyful song:

'All glory be to God on high,
And on the earth be peace;
Goodwill henceforth from heaven to men
Begin and never cease.'

7 The Christmas Story

The wise men

When Jesus was born in Bethlehem, a man named Herod was king. His palace was in the nearby city of Jerusalem.

Some men who studied the stars came to Jerusalem from lands to the east of the city. They had an important question for the people there: 'Where is the baby who is born to be your king? We have seen his star and have come to worship him.'

King Herod heard of their search, and he was at once angry. He hated anyone who threatened his power. So he called together his chief priests and teachers. 'You have studied the ancient writings of our people,' he said. 'They tell us that one day God will send us a special king—the Christ. Where will the Christ be born?'

'In Bethlehem,' they replied.

Then Herod called the travellers from the east to a secret meeting, and asked them what they knew about the star and when they had first seen it. When he had found out all they knew, he sent them to Bethlehem.

'Search for the king there,' he told them, 'and then come and tell me where he is.'

So the men left. They saw the star ahead of them. It stopped right over the place where the baby was. They went in and found the baby with his mother Mary.

Then they gave the gifts they had brought: gold and frankincense and myrrh.

Afterwards, they went back to their own land. In a dream, God told them not to go back to Herod, so they chose a different way home.

We Three Kings

We three kings of O-ri-ent are; Bear-ing gifts we tra-vel a-far. Field and foun-tain, moor and moun-tain, fol-low-ing yon-der star. O___ star of won-der, star of night, Star with roy-al beau-ty bright, West-ward lead-ing, still pro-ceed-ing, Guide us to thy per-fect light.

Melchior:
Born a king on Bethlehem plain,
Gold I bring to crown him again,
King for ever, ceasing never
Over us all to reign. (*Chorus*)

Caspar:
Frankincense to offer have I,
Incense owns a deity nigh;
Prayer and praising, all men raising,
Worship him, God most high! (*Chorus*)

Balthazar:
Myrrh is mine, its bitter perfume
Breathes a life of gathering gloom;
Sorrowing, sighing, bleeding, dying,
Sealed in the stone-cold tomb. (*Chorus*)

Glorious now behold him arise,
King and God and sacrifice,
Alleluia, alleluia,
Earth to the heavens replies. (*Chorus*)

8 A Nativity Scene

The Christmas story of the birth of Jesus is often called the Nativity. The word means 'birth'. Some people act out the story in Nativity plays at Christmas. Some set up a model of what happened in the story—a Nativity scene.

A stable

You will need

cardboard box

craft knife or strong scissors

marvin medium

white and brown acrylic paints

paintbrushes

straight twigs

strip of clear acetate film (overhead projector film is good)

gold card

sticky tape

pencil

1 Mix some marvin medium into each of the acrylic paint colours you are using. Brush over the stable. You will need to let each coat dry before adding more paint. Apply as many coats as you need to hide any writing on the box. Paint the outside dark and the inside a bit lighter.

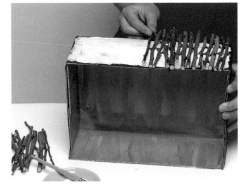

2 Put a thick layer of marvin medium on the 'roof' and lay straight twigs well into it. Leave to dry.

3 Draw a star on gold card and cut it out. Cut a strip of acetate and tape the star onto one end. Then tape the other end to the inside front of the stable.

9 Nativity Characters

You will need

thick card

thin white card

pencil

pencil crayons

scissors

plain and patterned paper in different colours

glue

paper clips

double-sided tape

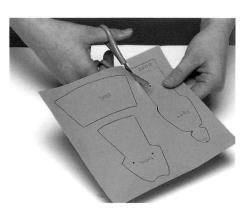

1 Copy the shapes at the back of this book onto thick card and cut them out. They are a figure, a tunic and a skirt shape.

2 Fold the thin white card in half and lay the figure shape on it, with the top of the head on the fold. Draw round this shape on white card to make as many figures as you need. Cut them out.

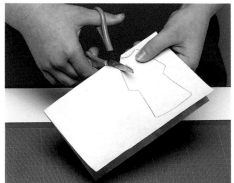

6 Draw round the shape for the tunic on a folded piece of coloured paper (to give a front and a back) and the shape for the skirt on a single piece of paper. Then cut them out. Make clothes for all the figures in this way.

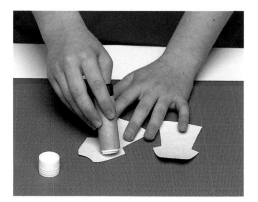

7 Wrap a skirt around the leg part of each figure and tape it in place. Spread glue on the wrong side of the tunic pieces, from the neck down to the bottom of the sleeves. Glue the front and back tunic pieces onto each figure.

3 Colour in the hands, feet and head. Colour the back and the front.

4 Open up the figure shape and put double-sided tape along the arms and the head on the inside. Fold the figure right side out and press the tape to stick the top part of the figure together.

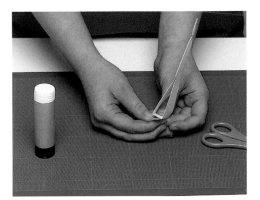

5 Fold the tabs at the bottom of each figure inwards and overlap them. Glue them together to make a base that will allow the figure to stay upright.

8 Add extra details if you wish. The belt is made by stitching a piece of yarn through the figure at waist level and tying a knot. The angel's wings are cut from a doily and taped on the back.

9 Make a manger from brown paper. Cut a rectangle 8 cm x 5 cm and fold in 15 mm along each side. Make snips as shown along the long creases to where they cross the short creases.

10 Fold up the sides and glue in place. Fill it with straw made from snipped paper and add a baby that you draw on thin card and cut out.

10 Christmas Gifts

Many stories are told of what Jesus did when he was grown-up. He spent his days telling people about God. He said that the God who made the world is kind, loving and forgiving. He said that the right way for people to live is to love God, and to be kind and forgiving to everyone around them. Many people listened to what Jesus had to say. Ever since, many, many people have tried to live as he taught. Here is a story of one of them.

The story of Saint Nicholas

Long ago, in the town of Myra, lived a man named Nicholas, He was the leader of the Christian community, and everyone knew him as a good and generous man.

In the town lived a poor family where there were three daughters. They were all old enough to get married. However, it was the tradition that a bride must bring a gift of money to her new family… and their father had none. No one wanted to marry them, and they were very sad.

Nicholas heard of their sorrow. He gathered together some gold coins. One dark night, he crept round to where the sisters lived, and threw the coins in through an open window.

The coins landed by the hearth, where the sisters had left their wet clothes to dry. In the morning, they found gold coins among their shoes and stockings—gifts that would enable them to get married and live happily.

Nicholas did many good deeds like this. He was so good, that people called him a saint: Saint Nicholas, or Santa Claus!

To this day many people hang up stockings on Christmas Eve, and on Christmas morning find that they have been filled with good things by a gift-giver who comes in secret.

Stockings

Here are Christmas stockings to decorate.

Will you hang a stocking at the foot of your bed on Christmas Eve, and will you find it full of gifts in the morning?

Will you be a gift-giver, and help fill a stocking secretly for someone you love?

You will need

long knitted socks in bright colours

bright yarns, buttons and beads

tapestry needle

1 Thread your needle with your first choice of bright yarn. Pull the two ends even. Push the needle through the folded cuff at a place where you want to put a tuft.

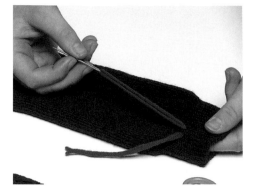

2 Take care to keep your other hand in the opening, so you don't stitch the opening up! Pull the needle through, leaving a tail of yarn about 10 cm long on the right side. Then push the needle back about 5 mm away.

3 Cut the thread to leave another tail about 10 cm long.

4 Tie the ends with a reef knot: wind the right thread over the left and pull snugly, then left over right and pull tight.

5 Snip the tails to leave a tuft about 2 cm long. Make tufts over the cuff in your choice of colours.

6 You can use the same method to tie on beads or buttons. Work from the inside to the outside and, using a single piece of yarn, thread a bead or button before taking the needle back to the inside. Tie off the ends on the inside and snip them to about 2 cm long.

12 The Christmas Tree

Decorating a tree with lights and pretty things is one of the best-loved Christmas traditions. Here is one story about why the tradition began.

The child and the fir tree

Long ago, a man named Boniface set off through Europe on a special journey. In the lands where he was travelling, people had never heard the story of Jesus. They did not believe in a God of love and gentleness. Some of the customs they followed were harsh and cruel.

One night, Boniface came across a gathering in the forest. People stood around a mighty oak tree. Tied to its trunk was a frightened child.

'What is going on?' Boniface wanted to know.

'The child must be killed, and offered as a sacrifice to our gods,' came the answer.

Boniface was dismayed. 'Please wait,' he asked. 'I believe that the great God of heaven and earth does not want this child to be killed. I want to tell you of a man named Jesus, who travelled this world hundreds of years ago showing people all the love and goodness of God.'

What he said made the people change their minds. When they had finished listening, they allowed Boniface to untie the child. They agreed to have the oak tree cut down.

By its roots was a little fir tree. 'The oak that you used for your old customs is gone,' he said. 'This tree is a symbol of your new belief, as followers of Jesus.'

13 Gingerbread Hearts

These simple tree decorations are spicy cookies. Their heart shape and their sweetness are a reminder of the love people can show each other.

Christmas is a time to remember that Jesus told his followers to love one another.

You will need

75 g brown sugar

30 ml golden syrup

15 ml black treacle

15 ml water

100 g margarine

1 tsp cinnamon

1 tsp ginger

250 g self-raising flour

extra flour

2 bowls

mixing spoon

rolling pin

drinking straws

baking parchment

heart-shaped cookie cutters

baking trays

wire rack

yarn

> ☺ *Ask a grown-up to help you cook. Have them preheat the oven to 160°C.*
>
> ☺ *Always wash your hands before you begin.*

1 Put the sugar, syrup, treacle, water and margarine into a bowl. Microwave on high for 2 minutes. Stir and microwave for 1 minute more.

5 Put a large sheet of baking parchment on a clean worksurface and sprinkle some extra flour on it. Roll the dough to 4 mm thick with a rolling pin.

6 Line a baking tray with baking parchment. Use a heart-shaped cutter to cut out your cookies. Lay them on the lined baking tray.

2 Put the flour and spices in another bowl and mix.

3 Stir the microwaved ingredients till they are liquid, then add this to the bowl of dry ingredients.

4 Stir till the mixture forms lumps, then use your hands to mix it so it forms a ball of dough.

7 Use a straw like a mini cutter to cut a hole in each cookie through which to thread your hanging loop. Press the end into the cookie and twist it slightly to lift out the tiny circle of dough (which will be pushed up into the straw).

8 Bake the cookies for 10 minutes or until they are just going dark at the edges. Ask a grown-up to lift them out of the oven and leave them on the tray till they are firm. Then lift them onto a wire rack to finish cooling.

9 Cut 30 cm lengths of yarn and fold them in half. Thread the looped end through the hanging hole of each heart, and then thread the dangling end through this loop. You can now use the ends to tie the cookie onto the tree.

14 Woven Hearts

These woven paper hearts are a traditional decoration. The colours chosen here stand for heaven and earth—a reminder of the Christian belief that Jesus was God's Son, come from heaven to show God's love on earth.

You will need

thick card

pencil and ruler

coloured paper

scissors

needle and yarn

1 Copy the shape shown at the back of this book onto thick card and cut it out. Mark the centre line as shown. Snip each side of the pencil line and pull away the thin curl of card in the middle.

2 Fold the coloured paper in half, wrong side showing. Lay the thick card with the flat end exactly on the crease and draw round it. Mark the centre line as well.

5 Next hold the folded end of the right-hand strip as you pull it through. Open up the fold and loop the strip over the upper strip of the left-hand shape.

6 Push the right-hand piece down so it settles into the slit on the left for the second part of the weaving. Take the top strip of the right-hand shape, open up the folded edge and loop it over the strip on the left.

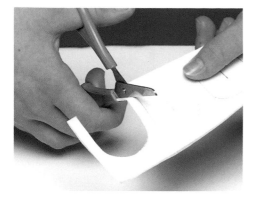

3 Cut out the coloured shape and snip ONCE along the centre line. Make shapes in different colours. Refold each one with the right side out.

4 Now begin weaving. Take two shapes of different colours and hold one in each hand with the folded ends facing. Push the lower strip of the shape in your right hand in between the two layers of the strip in your left.

7 Next, fold the edge of the right-hand strip closed again and push it through the left-hand shape. Jiggle the paper so the weaving fits snugly.

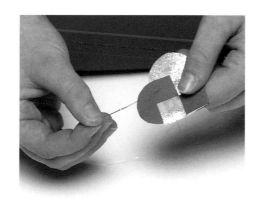

8 Thread a hanging loop through all thicknesses.

15 Christmas Cards

Many people send cards at Christmas—to tell their family and friends that they love and remember them, and perhaps to tell them some news.

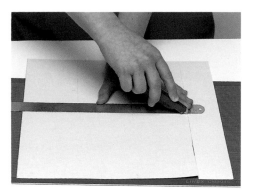

1 On the coloured card, measure a rectangle as tall as the size of card you want and three times as wide. Cut it out, using a craft knife against a ruler on a cutting mat.

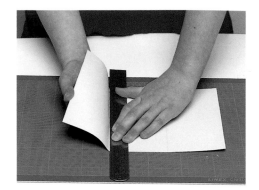

2 Mark the card into three panels along the top and bottom edges. Lay the ruler on the card to join them, and score lightly down this line with the craft knife. Fold the card up along this line, keeping the ruler in place to make the crease straight.

You will need

strong tracing paper or clear acetate film

stick of repositionable glue

craft knife and cutting mat

pencil and ruler

coloured card

acrylic paint

stencil brushes

block of polystyrene

thick needle

needle and thread

double-sided sticky tape

beads

scrap paper

3 Draw a stencil design for your card on the tracing paper or acetate film. Cut out the stencil design using the craft knife on the cutting mat.

4 Spread a little glue on the back of the stencil, then lay the stencil on the middle panel of the card where you want the design to go. Put some paint on a saucer and dab the stencil brush into it. Dab the paint on the stencil hole, taking care not to damage the edges of the stencil.

5 Peel the stencil away and let the card dry. Blot the back of the stencil on scrap paper before using it to make other cards in the same way.

6 Decide where you want to put beads on the card—like the glittery beads that add sparkle to the star, or the decorations on the tree. Open up the card and lay it on the polystyrene block. Use the thick needle to make holes where the beads will go.

7 Thread a thinner needle and tape the end of the thread on the inside of the card near a hole. Then bring the needle to the front through a hole, pick up a bead, and take the needle back through the hole. Take the needle to the next hole and do the same till the holes all have beads. Tape the end of the thread firmly on the inside.

8 Fold the front panel of the card inwards so that it covers the back of the middle panel. Tape it in place with double-sided tape.

16 Christmas News

At Christmas, it's good to have news about family and friends. Christians also like to hear again the news about Jesus and to share it with others.

Here is a Christmas carol which does just that.

Go, Tell It on the Mountain

Go tell it on the moun - tain, Ov - er the hills and ev - 'ry - where,___ Go tell it on the moun - tain That Je - sus Christ is born. While shep - herds kept their watch - ing Ov - er wander - ing flocks by night, Be - hold from out of hea - ven, There shone a ho - ly light.___

(Chorus)
And lo, when they had seen it,
They all bowed down and prayed,
They travelled on together
To where the babe was laid.
(Chorus)

17 Gift Wrapping

You can hide any shape of gift in this clever bag.

You will need

scissors

wrapping paper

sticky tape

hole punch

gift ribbon

gift, loosely wrapped in tissue paper

1 Cut a rectangle of wrapping paper large enough to go loosely round the gift, with plenty of extra top and bottom.

2 Lay the paper wrong-side up and fold the sides so they overlap in the middle. Tape the join and crease the side edges firmly.

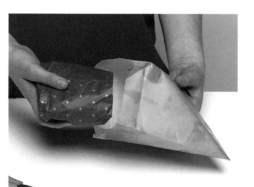

6 Unfold the top and put the gift inside. Then refold the top and tape shut.

7 Taking care not to damage the gift inside, punch a hole in each corner of the bag.

3 Fold a small triangle in at each of the bottom corners, and fold the lower edge up. Tape in place.

4 Now open up the top of the bag and bring the side creases together. Crease the new sides for a few centimetres down from the top.

5 Fold triangles in on these new sides and then fold down the top edge. Crease firmly but do not tape.

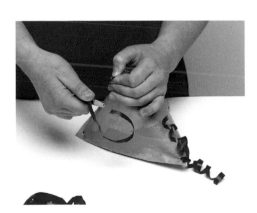

8 Thread gift ribbon through each hole and tie a knot. Tie it into bows or curl it.

18 Christmas Surprises

Just think of all the ways you can wrap gifts to make them look really festive.

It's a good idea to add a tag to each gift, saying who it is for and who it is from.

You will need

bright card

scissors

hole punch

gift ribbon

pen

1 Cut a simple shape from bright card.

2 Punch a hole in the tag.

3 Add your message.

4 Tie the tag in with the wrap.

We Wish You a Merry Christmas

We wish you a mer-ry Christ-mas, We wish you a mer-ry Christ-mas, We wish you a mer-ry Christ-mas And a hap-py New Year. *Good ti-dings we bring To you and your kin; We wish you a mer-ry Christ-mas And a hap-py New Year.*

Now bring us some figgy pudding,
Now bring us some figgy pudding,
Now bring us some figgy pudding,
And bring some out here. (*Chorus*)

For we all like figgy pudding,
We all like figgy pudding,
We all like figgy pudding,
So bring some out here. (*Chorus*)

And we won't go till we've got some,
We won't go till we've got some,
We won't go till we've got some,
So bring some out here. (*Chorus*)

19 Christingle

The Christingle is a traditional gift for children at Christmas. Many churches have special Christingle services, at which Christingles are given to children and everyone sings carols as the candles burn.

The different parts of the Christingle help tell the Christian story.

The orange stands for the world God made.

The sweets and fruits stand for all the good things the world provides, north, south, east and west.

The red ribbon stands for forgiveness. It is red like the colour of blood. When the baby Jesus grew up, he told people they must love and forgive one another. He said that they must do so because God loves and forgives people. Jealous enemies had Jesus put to death, nailed to a cross of wood. Still, as he hung bleeding, he forgave them. Christians believe that, in the same way, God forgives everyone.

The candle stands for Jesus. Christians believe that Jesus was God's Son, and he showed the world God's love. This love, they say, is light for the world.

You will need

an orange

double-sided tape

red ribbon

scissors

4 cocktail sticks

sweets and fruits

apple corer

kitchen foil (or Christmas foil)

candle

1 Wrap the double-sided tape around the middle of the orange.

2 Unpeel the backing and stick the ribbon in place on top of it. Tie a small knot to hold the ribbon tight and trim the ends.

3 Use the corer to make a candle-sized hole in the top of the orange.

4 Skewer sweets and fruits on the cocktail sticks and stick them into the orange.

5 Wrap foil around the bottom of the candle and push it firmly into the orange.

The story of the very first Christmas is the story of Jesus being born. For Christians, the message is the one that Jesus gave: that God loves people, and that people are happy when they love God and one another.

Bright paper chains link many different colours. They can be a reminder at Christmas of how many different kinds of people can be joined together in love.

Paper chains

You will need

coloured paper

ruler and pencil

sticky tape

1 With ruler and pencil, mark strips 2 cm x 15 cm on your paper.

2 Lay the ruler along the line and pull upwards on the paper to tear it into strips 15 cm wide. Then lay the ruler on the other lines to tear off strips 2 cm wide. Make strips in different colours.

3 Take one strip and tape it into a circle.

4 Thread another strip through it and tape that into a circle. Add more strips to make your chain as long as you like.

A Christmas prayer

God, our loving Father, help us remember the birth of Jesus, that we may share in the song of the angels, the gladness of the shepherds, and the wisdom of the wise men.

Close the door of hate and open the door of love all over the world.

Let kindness come with every gift and good desires with every greeting.

Deliver us from evil by the blessing which Christ brings and teach us to be merry with clean hearts.

May the Christmas morning make us happy to be your children and the Christmas evening bring us to our beds with grateful thoughts, forgiving and forgiven, for Jesus' sake. Amen.

Robert Louis Stevenson (1850–94)

templates for Nativity characters on page 9

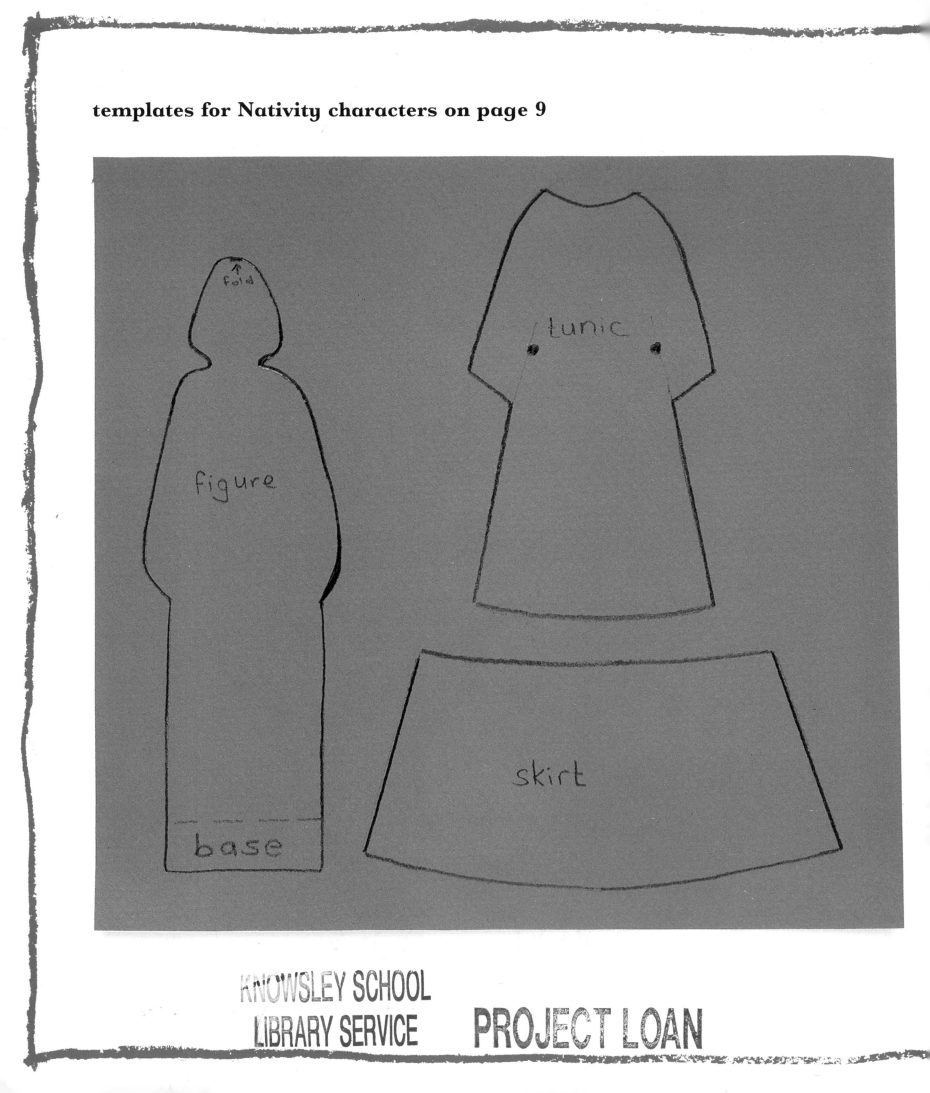